Wholeness Through

Healing
and
Forgiveness

Publisher:
Kenneth L. Fabbi
Lethbridge, Alberta, Canada
Email: FiveFoldCycle@gmail.com

Copyright © 2024 by Kenneth L. Fabbi

All rights reserved.

Unless otherwise indicated, all biblical quotations are taken from the New Revised Standard Version Bible, copyright © 1989 the Division of Christian Education of the National Council of the Churches of Christ in the United States of America. Used by permission. All rights reserved.

No part of this publication may be reproduced in any form, or by any means, electronic or mechanical, including photocopying, recording, or any information browsing, storage, or retrieval system, without permission in writing from the Author. Kenneth would welcome your communication at FiveFoldCycle@gmail.com.

ISBN:
Paperback: 978-1-7771066-5-2
eBook: 978-1-7771066-6-9

Subjects: *Healing Prayer - - Christianity - - Problem Solving - - Growth*

I. Title II. Fabbi, Kenneth L.

TABLE OF CONTENTS:

Acknowledgements 4

Preamble 5

Instructions 8

In Honor 10

Forgiveness 11

Forgiveness Prayer 15

Inner Healing Prayer 31

Psalm of Praise – Psalm 103 49

Notes 51

Appendix 'A' – Five Fold Cycle 56

Appendix 'B' – The Exchange 60

Appendix 'C' – Sisters of St. Francis of The Martyr St. George 62

ACKNOWLEDGEMENTS:

You know these booklets can't be made in isolation. There is always collaboration and personal sharing between the author and friends.

I want to thank Karla Conte, who gives of herself and shares from her heart, wanting that everyone finds deep inner peace and God's blessings. Thank you, Karla.

Sister M. Benedicta Bourke, FSGM, is the artist who shared her drawing of Jesus and the child. Sr. M. Benedicta put this inscription at the bottom of the picture which gives life to her drawing.

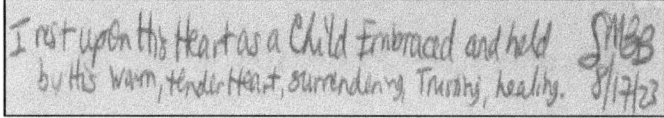

Thank you, Sr. M. Benedicta!

Sister's Order is described in Appendix 'C' - Sisters of St. Francis of The Martyr St. George.

Dennis Stroeve did his magic with the front cover, taking Sister's picture and the artwork necessary to make it work. Thank Dennis, always appreciate your friendship.

Wholeness Through

Healing and Forgiveness

My peers and I have often joke about all the good people who have 'junk-in-their-trunk.'

What do we mean by junk-in-their-trunk?

As we go through life we get hurt.

We pick up fears, confusion, anger, loneliness, guilt, shame and other negatives. In my book *Five Fold Cycle – Method of Healing Personal Hurt,* [1] I describe them as Roots of Bitterness.

Scripture describes it this way:

> *See to it that no one fails to obtain the grace of God; that no root of bitterness springs up and causes trouble, and through it many become defiled.*
> **Hebrews 12:15**

When we hold on to *junk in our trunk,* old negative thoughts and memories, both conscious and unconscious, tend to grow and develop. These hurts and traumas from the past become buttons that people can push. They are the underlying drives, emotions, feelings, motivations or decisions that run our lives.

Do you become easily angered? Do you turn to alcohol, drugs or unhealthy foods to get through the day? Does the thought of someone turn your stomach? These are examples of negatives.

When we realize that a situation is having a negative effect on our life, we have an opportunity to bring it to the Lord. He took everything on the Cross and from the Cross we receive His healing.

> *"Surely he has borne our infirmities and carried our diseases; yet we accounted him stricken, struck down by God, and afflicted. But he was wounded for our transgressions, crushed for our iniquities; upon him was the punishment that made us whole, and by his bruises we are healed."*
> Isaiah 53: 4-5

INSTRUCTIONS

It is recommend to take your time working through this booklet. For example, you could spend approximately 10 to 15 minutes reading one prayer in the morning and the following prayer in the evening for a period of 20 or 30 days.

If you find yourself reading though the prayer, do not be concerned. The prayers are meant to be used as a catalyst to bring up memories and experiences to allow for God's healing.

As you come across situations or memories that have hurt or are negative; stop reading and open up to prayer.

In prayer we give Jesus permission to enter into the wound, seeking the Father's pruning.

"I am the true vine, and my Father is the vinegrower. He removes every branch in me that bears no fruit. Every branch that bears fruit he prunes to make it bear more fruit."
John 15: 1-2

You will find that as you proceed through the prayers over the next days, that memories are healed and that you gain the inner peace that only Jesus can offer.

Each day will build on the previous day, thus you might not need to begin the prayer at the beginning but rather start where you left off.

Enjoy this season of prayer.

IN HONOR:

I would like to honor Fr. Robert Degrandis[2] and Betty Tapscott[3] who inspired this booklet. Both their ministries have closed. Back in the 1980's they taught and published similar material[4]. Their material was very useful in bringing healing and wholeness.

FORGIVENESS

> In the Our Father we find that God's forgiveness is equated with our forgiveness.
>
> *Forgive us as we forgive.*
> Matthew 6: 12; Luke 11: 4
>
> To receive God's grace of forgiveness we are required to forgive.
>
> **Forgiveness is an act of our will.**

Forgiveness allows us to move forward while unforgiveness cripples and torments us.

Forgiveness untangles the knots that bind us.

> *It is You who light my lamp; the LORD, my God, lights up my darkness.*
> **Psalm 18: 28**

When we forgive, we release the judgment and set people free. We are released and others are released from bondage when we forgive.

Forgiveness is a necessary component for inner healing; a pre-requisite so to speak.

"Therefore I say to you, whatever you ask when you pray, believe that you will have it, and it will be done for you. 25 And when you stand and pray, forgive, if you have

anything against any person, so that your Father who is in heaven may also forgive you your trespasses."
Mark 11: 24-25

As you read through the forgiveness prayer you will note it covers a wide range of areas; not all will apply to you. However, it will bring to mind significant people and areas of your life that are in need of healing and forgiveness.

Let the Holy Spirit move freely and guide your mind to persons or groups that you need to forgive.

As you pray it is recommended that you briefly visualize the person/situation and invite the Lord Jesus into the memory. Ask Jesus to give you what you need in that moment. Receive the healing and blessing. Ask for an infilling of the Holy Spirit and for the grace to bless those who have hurt you.

It is amazing what the Lord can do!

You can be assured that it is part of God's nature to heal your memories, emotions, feelings and mind.

FORGIVENESS PRAYER

PRAYER

Lord Jesus Christ, I know that You love me more than I love myself and want me to be whole.

I want to forgive everyone in my life. I look to You for the strength and grace to forgive, including those that are hardest to forgive. Come Holy Spirit.

FORGIVENESS OF SELF

I forgive myself for all my faults, failings, sins and omissions.

I forgive myself for breaking Your Commandments: for worshipping idols, taking Your name in vain, swearing, not keeping the sabbath holy, hurting my parents or children, abortion, gossiping, bullying, getting drunk, taking drugs, gluttony, sins against my purity, adultery, stealing, lying and for coveting my neighbors possessions.

Forgive me for my involvement in the occult, magic, reading horoscopes, Ouija boards, séances, fortune telling, and using lucky charms.

I forgive myself today and I thank You, Lord, for Your grace, mercy and extravagant love.[5]

FORGIVENESS OF MOTHER

I forgive my mother for her lack of love, affection, attention, understanding or support. I forgive her for hurting me, resenting me, her anger with me, her neglect, manipulation, control, yelling, jealousy, unrealistic expectations, unjust punishment, abuse and judgment.

Lord Jesus, I forgive her for the times she preferred my brothers and sisters over me. I forgive her for not protecting me.

I forgive her for the names she called me. I forgive her for comparing me to others or for saying I was a burden.

I forgive her for saying I was unwanted, an accident, a mistake or not the sex she expected. I forgive her for any abortions or attempted abortions.

Lord Jesus, I forgive her for drinking, taking drugs, pornography, arguing or fighting with my father or my siblings. I forgive her for any punishments and for any psychological, physical or sexual abuse.

I forgive her for not being there for me, not spending time with me and for not giving me her companionship.

I forgive her for being away from home, for being unfaithful and for divorcing my father.

FORGIVENESS OF FATHER

I forgive my father for his lack of love, affection, attention or support. I forgive him for hurting me, resenting me, his anger with me, unrealistic expectations, for punishing and judging me.

Lord Jesus, I forgive him for the times he preferred my brothers and sisters over me. I forgive him for his apathy and for not protecting me.

I forgive him for the names he called me. I forgive him for comparing me to the other children or saying I was a burden to the family.

I forgive him for saying I was unwanted, an accident, a mistake or not the sex he expected. I forgive him for his participation in any abortions.

Lord Jesus, I forgive him for drinking, taking drugs, pornography, arguing and fighting with my mother or my siblings. I forgive him for any psychological, physical or sexual abuse and punishments.

I forgive him for not being there for me, not spending time with me, not giving me his companionship and for not defending me.

I forgive him for being away from home, for divorcing my mother, or for any unfaithfulness.

FORGIVENESS OF SIBLINGS

I forgive my brothers and sisters. I forgive those who hated me, rejected me, lied about me, stole from me, resented me, bullied me and competed for my parents' love.

Lord Jesus, I forgive my brothers and sisters who hurt me, treated me harshly and made my life unpleasant. I forgive them for rejecting me and for their lack of understanding. I forgive them for psychologically, physically or sexually harming me.

FORGIVENESS OF SPOUSE

I forgive my spouse for their lack of love, affection, intimacy, consideration, time, support, attention and communication.

Lord Jesus, I forgive my spouse for their faults and failures, weaknesses, selfishness, hurtful words and actions. I forgive my spouse for harming me or others.

Especially I forgive my spouse for failure to commit to our vows. I forgive my spouse for any unfaithfulness, watching pornography or for psychologically, physically or sexually abusing me. Help me to forgive and heal me, Lord.

FORGIVENESS OF CHILDREN

I forgive my children for their lack of honor, respect, obedience, love, attention, support, warmth, and understanding.

Lord Jesus, I forgive my children for their sins, bad habits, negative words, judgment, deceit, selfishness, absence, manipulation, abuse and for not living a Christian faith.

FORGIVENESS OF SON OR DAUGHTER IN-LAW

I forgive my son or daughter in-law and other relatives by marriage, for their negative words, thoughts, judgment, actions or omissions and abuse which have injured my family and myself.

Lord Jesus, I forgive them for their lack of love, cooperation and support. I forgive them for their interference in any family relationships.

FORGIVENESS OF RELATIVES

I forgive my aunts, uncles, grandmothers, grandfathers and cousins who hurt me or my family. I forgive them for interfering in my family, for being controlling or possessive, for their lack or support, judgement, omissions, gossip and slander.

Lord Jesus, I forgive them for causing confusion or division. I forgive all who had a negative influence on me and my family.

FORGIVENESS OF CO-WORKERS

I forgive my co-workers for their interference, judgement, insults, for being disagreeable or for making work miserable.

Lord Jesus, I forgive those who were uncooperative or who pushed their work off on me. I forgive those who used me, stole, gossiped or who tried to take my job. I forgive my co-workers for their lack of compassion.

FORGIVENESS OF NEIGHBORS

I forgive my neighbors for their lack of cooperation, being careless, their noise, not caring for their property, for their pets, trash and vehicles.

Lord Jesus, I forgive them for, words spoken, prejudice, judgement, slander, stealing, doing drugs, disruptions, unfriendliness and for running down the neighborhood.

FORGIVENESS OF PASTOR/ PRIEST, RELIGIOUS AND CLERGYMAN

I forgive my priest, pastor, clergyman, congregation and my church for their pettiness, judgment, lack of friendliness, affirmation or support and for their lack of community.

Lord Jesus, I forgive them for not including me or inviting me to serve and for any other hurt they have inflicted.

I forgive them for any sexual, emotional, physical or psychological abuse past or present done to me or anyone else. I forgive them that my heart be healed and my anger subsided.

FORGIVENESS OF DOCTORS AND PROFESSIONALS

I forgive all professional people who have hurt me in any way: doctors, nurses, inspectors, lawyers, policemen, fireman, counselors, hospital staff or others.

Lord Jesus, I forgive each of them today and ask that you bless them and open them to your healing.

FORGIVENESS OF EMPLOYER

I forgive my employer for not respecting me, not paying a fair wage and for not appreciating my work.

Lord Jesus, I forgive them for being unkind and unreasonable, for being angry and for not promoting me or complimenting me on my work.

I FORGIVE MY TEACHERS

I forgive my school teachers and instructors. I forgive them for unjust punishment, humiliation, insults, abuse and for treating me unjustly or poorly.

Lord Jesus, I forgive them for making fun of me, calling me names, not promoting or protecting me, and for keeping me in detention after school.

I FORGIVE MY FRIENDS

Lord Jesus, I forgive my friends who let me down, borrowed or stole, did not support me, spoke unkindly, gossiped about me, passed judgment or who lost contact with me.

I forgive them for being unavailable and for not noticing when I needed their help.

I FORGIVE THAT ONE PERSON WHO HURT ME THE MOST

Lord Jesus, I need the grace to forgive! I especially ask for the grace to forgive that one person in life who has hurt me the most.

Lord Jesus, it is hard to forgive, especially the one whom I consider my greatest enemy, the one who has hurt me the most.

Lord, I forgive that one person who hurt me most.

Thank You, Jesus, that with Your extravagant love and help I am free and I can forgive.

Lord Jesus, forgive me for my negative words when I said that "I will never forgive." I revoke the curse in the name of Jesus.

Lord Jesus, I ask for You to bless those who have hurt me.

Holy Spirit, healer, fill me with light and let every dark area of my mind be enlightened.

Amen.

INNER HEALING PRAYER

The following prayer covers significant periods of life. You are invited to open memories to Christ's healing. We call this inner healing (healing of memories). Ask Jesus to heal your memories or painful trauma. It is an intimate time between you and the Lord.

You may use the prayer template on the following page.

Praying Through Life's Hurts
Using the *Five Fold Cycle*

Becoming God Focused:
Father, Emmanuel, I thank you that you are God with us and I invite you into

_____ .

(Outline the problem, memory, concern etc.).

Identify:
Come Holy Spirit, give me understanding and enlighten my heart. Reveal any roots, moments, thoughts, decisions or wounds that need healing *(Listen for the Holy Spirit's guidance).*

Clean:
Lord Jesus, knowing that you took everything on the Cross, I place _____ at the foot of your cross. Take away any negatives and cleanse me.

Fill:
Lord Jesus, I ask you for an infilling of the Holy Spirit. Renew my Body, Mind, Soul, and Spirit.

Thank the Lord:
I thank you God the Father for life, for renewing me and pruning away the brokenness that I might be whole.

Bless you and praise you for ever!
Amen   (Appendix 'A' – Five Fold Cycle)

WALKING BACK IN TIME

Thank You God the Father for Your Son, Jesus. You sent Your Son Jesus to be an exchange on the cross, where He took not only my sins, but made provisions for me (spiritual, physical, and material) for time and eternity. (Reference Appendix 'B' – The Exchange.)

I thank You Jesus that in You I am made completely whole: mind, body, soul and spirit.

I thank you Lord that you are God with me, God Emmanuel.

> *"The Lord your God will be with you wherever you go."*
> Joshua 1: 9

Walk back in time with me now, through every second of my life. Please heal me and make me whole.

> *"He heals the brokenhearted and binds up their wounds."*
> **Psalm 147: 3**

> *"May the God of peace himself sanctify you entirely, and may your spirit, soul and body be kept complete and blameless at the coming of our Lord Jesus Christ."*
> **1 Thessalonians 5: 23**

GENERATIONS

In scripture it talks about the effects of sin going back to the third and fourth generations.[6] I repent of their sins and I ask you now Lord Jesus, to break the effect of generational sin from my life and heal any harmful genetic flaws.

CONCEPTION AND THE WOMB

Jesus, scripture says You knew me before I was born.[7] Thank You for giving me life! Thank You, Lord Jesus, for being there and loving me.

If fear, rejection, confusion, stress, feeling unloved or any other negative power was transmitted to me while in my mother's womb through broken relationships, pre-marital sex, divorce, trauma, alternative methods of conception, adoption or gender rejection, heal me and cleanse me of those things.

In pregnancy, many have reached out to the occult or fortune telling for good-luck or influence, Lord, remove any contamination.

Lord Jesus, come into this very foundational moment of my life, with Your extravagant love and make me whole.

EARLY YEARS

Lord, come into my early childhood years; a time of play, innocence and imagination. I invite you Lord into every second of my life to fill it with Your extravagant love.

In the brokenness of the world and families, I may have been separated from my parents or families because of divorce, separation, sickness, conflict, death, war or government policies. Some were born into large families and did not receive the love that was needed. Some were mistreated, abused and abandoned.

I forgive my mother or father for intentionally denying me of having a full relationship with my other parent. I forgive any persons who denied me a relationship with my family members.

Lord Jesus, go back and fill every void with Your love. We know that You are the parent for the orphan and the Father for the fatherless.[8]

Remove every hurt – heal every trauma. Take away all fears of darkness, bugs, animals, falling, separation, being alone or lost.

Thank You, Jesus, for healing me and making me whole.

SCHOOL DAYS

Jesus, walk me back to school days when I was so young and innocent. I was often afraid, shy, and uncertain, leaving home to go to school. I invite You into those memories Lord. I remember the teacher who embarrassed me, the classmates who bothered me; please heal those hurts.

Those times were not without fears and confusion: fear of the first school days, fear of fitting in, fear of speaking, or fear of failures.

Lord Jesus, go back and fill every void with Your love; enter into each memory and heal the hurts and trauma.

Thank You Lord for Your extravagant love.

MOTHER

Jesus, I thank You for my mother. Be the conduit between my mother and I, fill any void in her love.

I may have experienced a lack of mother's love, due to large families, mothers' sickness, separation and death. Fill those voids, Lord.

Lord Jesus, forgive me for my failures and the ways I hurt my mother and I forgive her for any way she hurt or fell short of giving me the love and care that I needed.

Lord Jesus, go back and fill every void with Your love. Enter into each memory and heal the hurts and trauma.

Thank You Lord for Your extravagant love.

FATHER

Jesus, I thank You for my father. Be the conduit between my father and I and fill any void in his love.

If I experienced a lack of father's love, due to his focus on work, sickness, separation and death, fill those voids, Lord.

Lord Jesus, I forgive my father for any way he hurt me or fell short of giving me the love and care that I needed. Please forgive me for my failures and the ways I hurt my father.

Lord Jesus, go back and fill every void with Your love. Lord, enter into each memory and heal the hurts and trauma.

SIBLINGS

Jesus, thank you for my brothers and sisters. Lord, I invite you into the times when there was competition, anger, jealousy, or resentment.

Lord Jesus, heal and mend every broken relationship. Forgive me for my failures and the ways I hurt my brothers and sisters and I forgive them for any way they hurt or fell short of giving me their love and care.

Lord Jesus, go back and fill every void with Your love. I invite you into each memory and ask you to heal the hurts and trauma.

TEENAGE YEARS

Jesus, walk me back to my teenage years in junior high school and high school. There were many positive and negative experiences.

As You guide me through the memories, take away the pain and hurt. Lord, I remember times of hurt, feeling afraid and confused, guilt, humiliation, peer pressure, embarrassment, fear and failure. Cleanse these hurts with Your extravagant love.

If I was slighted because of

race, looks, size, or poverty, enter into each memory.

Lord Jesus, go back and fill every void with Your love. Lord, enter into each memory and heal the hurts and trauma.

LEAVING HOME

Jesus, there were new issues as I started to leave home: fears, frustrations, loneliness or hurts. I had dreams of college, university, careers, professions and marriage. Many times, I was disappointed.

Lord Jesus, go back and fill every void with Your love. Lord enter into each memory and heal the hurts, disappointments and trauma.

MARRIAGE & RELATIONSHIPS

Jesus, my romantic relationships and/or marriage were at times both beautiful and problematic. Each new person offered an excitement and learning, thank You for them.

Lord Jesus, please take the hurt from failures in my relationships. Forgive me for my failures and the ways I hurt my partners, and I forgive them for any way they hurt me or fell short of giving me the love and sensitivity that I needed.

Lord Jesus, go back and fill every void with Your love. Lord enter into each memory and heal the hurts and trauma.

Lord Jesus, through Your extravagant love, heal and mend every broken relationship and every painful memory.

CHILDREN

Jesus, thank You for the blessing of children. As a parent, I have often felt conflicting feelings of joy in their successes and failure or guilt when they failed.

I have lost my temper, punished, controlled, been over possessive, manipulated and spoken words without love.

Lord Jesus, go back and fill every void with Your extravagant love. Heal every hurt that was caused. Forgive my failures and renew our relationships.

EVENTS & TRAUMA

Jesus, as I have gone through life there have been accidents, sickness, health problems, loss, change and trauma. I ask You to enter into these events.

Lord Jesus, go back in time and heal the memories and the hurts. Set me free from any trauma, fear, loss or hurt; renew my heart and my mind.

Lord, if there was abuse in any form: sexual, emotional, physical, psychological etc., heal me.

Lord Jesus, take away any sorrow, grief, loss or mourning. Give me Your joy and Your peace that passes all understanding[9].

THANK YOU, LORD

Jesus, thank You for walking back through every moment of my life. Thank You for healing all my hurts, painful memories, trauma, fears and for setting me free.

Lord Jesus, thank You for filling me with Your extravagant love, that I might love You. Help me to love myself, love others and to love like You love.

Give me a new joy. Holy Spirit give me Your peace.

Lord, I give you permission to heal the inner parts of my mind, heart, soul and spirit and ask You to make me whole.

Lord, please bless all the people who passed through my mind.

Forgive them, renew them and bring them closer to you.

Thank You, Lord Jesus. Thank You for going deep into the recesses of my mind and heart. Thank you for cleansing and healing me.

I praise You.

Amen.

PSALM OF PRAISE

¹ Bless the LORD, O my soul, and all that is within me, bless his holy name. ² Bless the LORD, O my soul, and do not forget all his benefits— ³ who forgives all your iniquity, who heals all your diseases, ⁴ who redeems your life from the Pit, who crowns you with steadfast love and mercy, ⁵ who satisfies you with good as long as you live so that your youth is renewed like the eagle's. ⁶ The LORD works vindication and justice for all who are oppressed. ⁷ He made known his ways to Moses, his acts to the people of Israel. ⁸ The LORD is merciful and gracious, slow to anger and abounding in steadfast love. ⁹ He will not always accuse, nor will he keep his anger forever. ¹⁰ He does not deal with us according to our sins nor repay us according to our iniquities. ¹¹ For as the heavens are high above the earth, so great is his steadfast love toward those who fear him; ¹² as far as the east is from the west, so far he removes our transgressions from us. ¹³ As a father

has compassion for his children, so the LORD has compassion for those who fear him. ¹⁴ For he knows how we were made; he remembers that we are dust. ¹⁵ As for mortals, their days are like grass; they flourish like a flower of the field; ¹⁶ for the wind passes over it, and it is gone, and its place knows it no more. ¹⁷ But the steadfast love of the LORD is from everlasting to everlasting on those who fear him, and his righteousness to children's children, ¹⁸ to those who keep his covenant and remember to do his commandments. ¹⁹ The LORD has established his throne in the heavens, and his kingdom rules over all. ²⁰ Bless the LORD, O you his angels, you mighty ones who do his bidding, obedient to his spoken word. ²¹ Bless the LORD, all his hosts, his ministers who do his will. ²² Bless the LORD, all his works, in all places of his dominion. Bless the LORD, O my soul.

Psalm 103: 1-22

NOTES:

[1] Fabbi. Kenneth L., *Five Fold Cycle – Method of Healing Personal Hurt: Healing Life's Hurts*, Lethbridge, Alberta, Canada, Kenneth L. Fabbi, 2019.

[2] Fr. Robert DeGrandis (1932 – 2018) was a member of the Society of St. Joseph. He was involved in a full-time teaching, leadership training and healing ministry around the world. He was a member of the Association of Christian Therapists.

[3] Betty Stevens Tapscott (1933) now age 91, ministered in the USA, Canada, England and Costa Rica. Through her ministry she brought a message of Jesus' healing and wholeness.

[4] Tapscott, Betty & DeGrandis, Father Robert S.S.J. *Forgiveness & Inner Healing*, 1980. (Out of Print)

[5] <u>**Extravagant Love**</u>:

Consider the kind of extravagant love the Father has lavished on us— He calls us children of God! It's true; we are His beloved children. And in the same way the world didn't recognize Him, the world does not recognize us either.

When we feel like we are not good enough to be loved by God, we should remember that God's love is greater than our doubts. We must silence the sounds of condemnation so we can hear the voice of God's loving assurance and remember that He has selected us to be part of His family.
1 John 3: 1 - The Voice (VOICE)

6 Third and Fourth Generations:

You shall not bow down to them or serve them, for I the LORD your God am a jealous God, punishing children for the iniquity of parents to the third and fourth generation of those who reject me
Deuteronomy 5: 9

'The LORD is slow to anger and abounding in steadfast love, forgiving iniquity and transgression, but by no means clearing the guilty, visiting the iniquity of the parents upon the children to the third and the fourth generation.'
Numbers 14: 18

7 Knew me before I was born:

"Before I formed you in the womb I knew you, and before you were born I consecrated you; I appointed you a prophet to the nations."
Jeremiah 1: 5

8 <u>Parent for the orphan and the father for the fatherless</u>:

Father of orphans and protector of widows is God in his holy habitation.

Psalm 68: 5

Religion that is pure and undefiled before God the Father is this: to care for orphans and widows in their distress and to keep oneself unstained by the world.
James 1: 27

9 <u>Your joy and Your peace that passes all understanding</u>:

And the peace of God, which surpasses all understanding, will guard your hearts and your minds in Christ Jesus.
Philippians 4: 7

[9] As the Father has loved me, so I have loved you; abide in my love. [10] If you keep my commandments, you will abide in my love, just as I have kept my Father's commandments and abide in his love. [11] I have said these things to you so that my joy may be in you, and that your joy may be complete.
John 15: 9-11

May the God of hope fill you with all joy and peace in believing, so that you may abound in hope by the power of the Holy Spirit.
Romans 15: 13

[10] Derek Prince Ministries of Canada, Suite #178, 1111 Davis Drive, Unit 23, Newmarket, Ontario, L3Y 9E5.
Phone: 1- 647-217-8932

Appendix 'A'

THE FIVE FOLD CYCLE
METHOD OF HEALING PERSONAL HURT*

Healing Life's Hurts

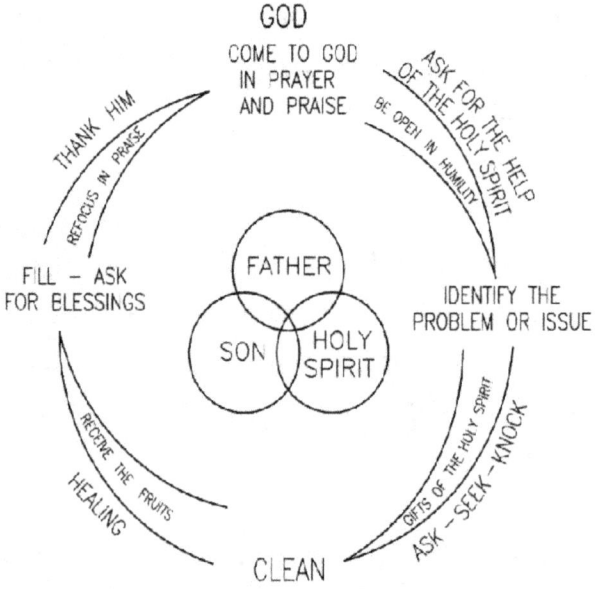

This was to fulfill what had been spoken through the prophet Isaiah, "He took our infirmities and bore our diseases." Mt. 8:17 & Is. 53:4-5

*Fabbi, Kenneth L., *Five Fold Cycle - Method of Healing Personal Hurt, Healing Life's Hurts*. Kenneth Fabbi, Canada, 2019

FIVE FOLD CYCLE

Method Of Healing Personal Hurt

(A PROBLEM SOLVING METHOD)

I have started training people to do housecleaning. It goes like this:

When we are hurt, there are 3 negative reactions:

1. Unforgiveness - Anger, bitterness, resentment and the like is the first major problem.

2. Guilt - which is self-pity, uncertainty, not forgiving self, worry, anxiety, tension caused by worry is the second problem.

3. Depression - This is a symptom of the previous two and therefore when you deal with #1 and #2, depression leaves on its own.

Process:

The answer to how to deal with these is easy if you believe in Christ's help. It goes through a Five Fold Cycle.

FIVE FOLD CYCLE
Method Of Healing Personal Hurt

1. Become God Focused: Focus on God in prayer praise and thanksgiving. Ask for the gifts of the Spirit, which include wisdom, knowledge and understanding. Be humble and penitent.

2. Identify: Identify problems and be specific. Ask for wisdom and knowledge from the Lord. Look for specific sources for the problems and expand on them. Often problems interconnect, so make sure to separate and individualize them. Do things one at a time. It is a process of healing.

3. Clean: Do something.

CLEANSE
- Forgive where forgiveness is needed.
- Forgive others, God and self
- Bind any spiritual involvement.
- Confess and ask for cleansing.
- Give up the problem to the Lord, e.g.: anxiety / worry / etc.
- Ask the Lord to take it away.
- It is often important to actually follow through by personal contact with the parties involved. Be sensitive to the Lord's direction in this matter.
- It is good to take these matters to the Communion Table and repeat the process.

What we are doing in this section is gradually nibbling away at the problem areas. Remember you cannot deal with depression because it is a symptom and often very global in nature.

4. Fill:

BLESSING

- Ask for the in-filling of the Holy Spirit.
- Ask for the contrasting good characteristics.
- Ask for the blessings and gifts to fill the space left when you cleansed yourself in # 3.
- Prayer and Scripture reading are important.
- Make sure to ask for blessings for others you have cleansed. They also need the gifts and blessings.
- Ask the Lord to heal the hurt.
- Take it to Communion or Eucharist.

If you clean the areas/problems and do nothing to replace them with positives, there is a high probability that you can slip back into the same old routines. You must fill the place that has been cleaned up, with the good things from God through his Holy Spirit.

5. Go Back to # 1. Stop focusing on yourself. Thank the Lord.

Appendix 'B'

THE EXCHANGE

There was an exchange on the Cross of Jesus. Let me explain this by quoting from Derek Prince[10]:

If you have a need or problem in your life, there is only one place and one place alone where you must go to find the provision or God's solution. And that one place is the Cross of Jesus.

Through what Jesus accomplished by His death on the Cross, every provision of God for you; spiritual, physical, material, for time or eternity has been made available.

Simply: God laid on Jesus the iniquity of us all. (*Iniquity* could also be translated *rebellion*. Rebellion and all the consequences and judgments that come upon rebellion.) Our rebellion, the rebellion of the entire sin cursed Adamic race, came upon Jesus upon the Cross, by divine appointment.

That is the negative part of the exchange. The positive side is that in return, all the good that was due to the sinless obedience of Jesus might be available to us. God visited upon Jesus the evil due to us that in return he might make available to us the good due to Jesus.

Appendix 'C'
Sisters of St. Francis of The Martyr St. George

Sisters of St. Francis of the Martyr St. George is a congregation of religious women founded in Germany in 1869. Our charism is first to receive then make Christ's Merciful Love visible in the world.

We serve in Germany, the Netherlands, Japan, Indonesia, Brazil, Albania, Rome and Assisi, Italy, and the United States. The American Province is based in Alton, Illinois (near St. Louis), serving the poor and needy, specifically in education, health care, pastoral work, and care of priests.

As Franciscans, we are known for our joy, and love of Christ Crucified, the Incarnation and the Holy Eucharist. Our prayer life flows from the Pierced Side of Christ starting with daily Mass, adoration of the Blessed Sacrament, and Stations of the Cross.

We just celebrated serving 100 years in the U.S.

You can learn more and contact us at www.altonfranciscans.org

KENNETH L. FABBI PUBLICATIONS

Five Fold Cycle – Method of Healing Personal Hurt
Sub-titled: ***Heal Life's Hurts***
February 28, 2019 - Third Publication
Five Fold Cycle teaches how to pray for Inner Healing and empowers people to pray and watch for God's healing in their lives and in the lives of people around them.
Hard Cover ISBN: 978-0-9952039-0-7
Paperback ISBN: 978-0-9952039-1-4
eBook ISBN: 978-0-9952039-2-1
Spanish Paperback ISBN: 978-0-9952039-7-6
Spanish eBook ISBN: 978-0-9952039-8-3

You Can Minister Spiritual Gifts
by Thomas W. Roycroft
It was re-published: March 02, 2019
Paperback ISBN: 978-0-9952039-3-8
eBook ISBN: 978-0-9952039-4-5
Both this book and the previous book are good teaching tools. Prayer Group members and myself re-edit Thomas W. Roycroft's material. He developed the book as a course on the Gifts of the Holy Spirit, encouraging people to activate the Gifts and live a life in God's Holy Ghost.

SCRIPTURE HEALING: How to ~~***Play***~~ ***Pray Scripture***

It was published: August, 2019

Scripture Healing: How to ~~Play~~ Pray Scripture became a publishing project because Kenneth found truth in the fact, that the Word of God Heals!

People who apply scripture to their life and pray with scripture get healed. As we read and take the Scripture into our mind and heart, God the Father uses it to transform us.

This booklet is meant to walk you through a collection of Scriptures from the Holy Bible. Each Scripture offers a truth. Many of the Scriptural passages offer insight into healing and God's design.

Kenneth encourages you to play and experiment with these ideas and share them with your friends.

Paperback ISBN: 978-0-9952039-5-2
eBook ISBN: 978-0-9952039-6-9
Spanish Paperback ISBN: 978-0-9952039-9-0
Spanish eBook ISBN: 978-1-7771066-0-7

Powered by the Gift of Tongues
It was published: September, 2023.
God the Father wants to give you his Holy Spirit, (Luke 11: 13 & 2 Corinthians 5: 5). The Father's gift is *one gift* and that is the Holy Spirit. In the Spirit resides many manifestations, Tongues being one of them. St. Paul makes it clear that it is desirable to have the Gift of Tongues: *"I would like everyone of you to speak in tongues..."* (1 Corinthians 13: 5). The conclusion that we can draw is that, Christians should be asking our Father for His gift.
Paperback ISBN: 978-1-7771066-1-4
eBook ISBN: 978-1-7771066-2-1

Five Fold Cycle – Workbook: Method of Healing Personal Hurt
It was published: May 13, 2024.
The Workbook expands the original text and outlines a Method of Healing Personal Hurt through the Five Fold Cycle. Through Scripture Studies, Study Notes and Workshops, students learn and implement the healing process, learning to open to God, listen to the Holy Sprit and receive the healing available through Jesus' death on the Cross.
Paperback ISBN: 978-1-7771066-3-8
eBook ISBN: 978-1-7771066-4-5

www.ingramcontent.com/pod-product-compliance
Lightning Source LLC
Chambersburg PA
CBHW072136070526
44585CB00016B/1711